How to
be fine about
PLANNING
A WEDDING

ICE HOUSE BOOKS

Published by Ice House Books

Copyright © 2020 Ice House Books

Illustrated and designed by Kayleigh Hudson
Written and compiled by Zulekhá Afzal & Raphaella Thompson

Ice House Books is an imprint of Half Moon Bay Limited
The Ice House, 124 Walcot Street, Bath, BA1 5BG
www.icehousebooks.co.uk

All rights reserved. No part of this book may be reproduced, stored in
a retrieval system, communicated or transmitted in any form or by any
means without prior written permission from the publisher.

The material in this publication is of the nature of general comment only,
and does not represent professional advice.

ISBN 978-1-912867-77-6

Printed in China

TO:

FROM:

Welcome to planning your

WEDDING!

Where you'll whack someone over the head with your guest list next time you're asked how it's going.

The highest
happiness on earth
is the happiness
of marriage.

William Lyon Phelps

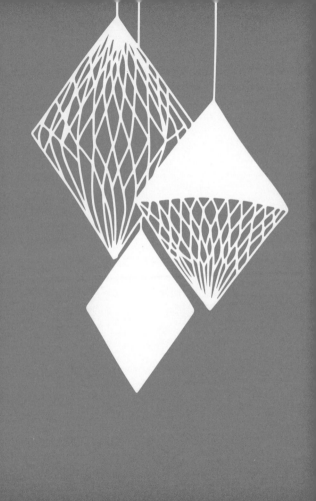

STAGES OF PLANNING A WEDDING

STAGE ONE
Tell EVERYONE you're engaged.

STAGE TWO
Pinterest is your new best friend.

STAGE THREE
Wait ... wedding's cost *how much?!*

STAGE FOUR
Cue everyone else's opinions
on your special day.

STAGE FIVE
F**k it. Let's elope!

The only part of the wedding planning I'm interested in is the cake tasting.

To get the full value of joy you must
have someone to divide it with.

Mark Twain

If I cry at my wedding,
it'll be because I'm
overjoyed the planning
is finally over.

I hope my wedding's as good as what I pinned on Pinterest.

THERE IS
NOTHING
LIKE
PLANNING
A WEDDING
TO MAKE
YOU WANT
TO PUNCH
EVERY
PERSON
YOU MEET.

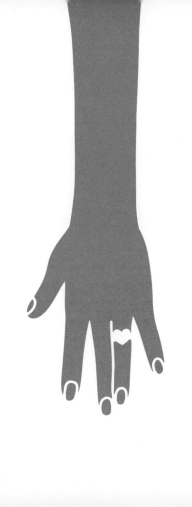

LISTEN

— SMILE —

AGREE.

(Then do whatever you were going to do anyway.)

Love is of all passions
the strongest, for it
attacks simultaneously
the head, the heart,
and the sense.

Lao Tzu

A happy marriage is the
union of two forgivers.

Ruth Graham

This'll be easy!

Yeah, I don't want to
do this anymore.

Sooo, we can't invite **this** person
without inviting **that** person ...

It's out there in the world.
No going back now.

Oh, that's fine, we didn't need
you to RSVP. We just added
that to the invite
COS IT'S FUNNY!

Whatever our souls are made of,
his and mine are the same.

Emily Brontë
Wuthering Heights

I love you more
than I love cake.

Thank you for
marrying me
despite the person
I've become during
the planning.

However you get there,
just make sure you
get there on time.

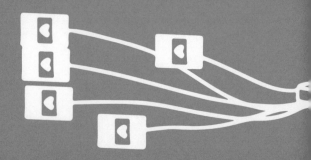

Coming together
is a beginning;
keeping together
is progress;
working together
is success.

Henry Ford

AND THE
ADVENTURE
BEGINS ...

Grow old along with me;
the best is yet to be.

Robert Browning

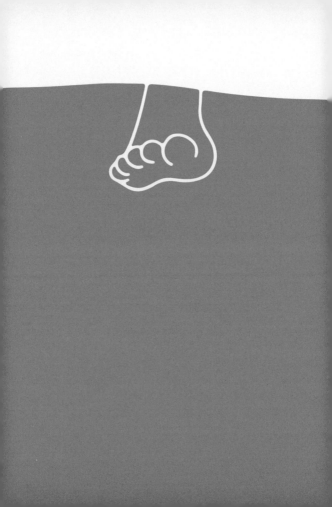

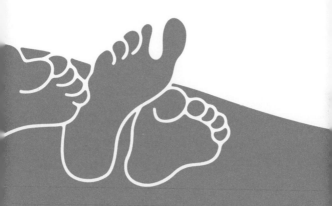

MARRIAGE
· · · · · · · · · · · · · · · · · · · ·
An endless sleepover
with your favourite weirdo.

I'm on a seafood

diet for my

wedding ...

I see food,

I eat it.

The future looks better
than I could have hoped for,

now that you're
going to be part of it.

WEDDING PLAN

WINE

— SLEEP —

REPEAT

I wonder if I'll be the one who always
remembers our anniversary,
or the one who always forgets it …

I'm so ready
to shout
"WHAT?!"
at each other
from opposite
ends of
the house.

I would rather share one
lifetime with you

than face all the ages of
this world alone.

J.R.R. Tolkien
The Lord of the Rings

They say marriages are made in heaven. But so is thunder and lightning.

Clint Eastwood

*I love you more today
than yesterday.*

Yesterday you really got on my nerves.

Love is composed of a single soul
inhabiting two bodies.

Aristotle

People are WEIRD.

When we find someone with

weirdness that is compatible

with ours, we team up and

CALL IT LOVE.

Dr. Seuss

Love is the seventh sense
which destroys all other six senses.

Remember this,
that very little is needed to
make a happy life.

Marcus Aurelius

STAGES OF CHOOSING YOUR WEDDING PARTY

STAGE ONE
Piece. Of. CAKE.

STAGE TWO
Nope.

STAGE THREE
I haven't spoken to them in five years,
but I was in their wedding party
so I can't not ask them, can I?

STAGE FOUR
At this rate, the whole guest list
will be in the wedding party ...

STAGE FIVE
... I'm going to bed now.

Thanks for not putting
the ring in my food
when you proposed.

Yeah ... I definitely
would have eaten it.

It takes as much energy to *wish*

as it does to *plan.*

Eleanor Roosevelt

BEING MARRIED

is like having a

best friend

… who doesn't remember anything you say.

How many candles is TOO many candles?

It is such a happiness
when good people get together
- and they always do.

Jane Austen
Emma

Marriage is an attempt to solve problems together which you didn't even have when you were on your own.

Eddie Cantor

*Keep your eyes wide
open before marriage,*

half shut afterwards.

Benjamin Franklin

I promise to still grab your arse
when we're old and wrinkly.

The longest sentence you can
form with two words is: I do.

H. L. Mencken

You know you're

in love when you

can't fall asleep

because reality is

finally better

than your dreams.

Dr. Seuss

Being deeply loved
by someone gives you

STRENGTH,

while loving someone
deeply gives you

COURAGE.

Lao Tzu

REMEMBER

to plan the wedding
you've always wanted,

• • • • • • • • • • • • • • • • • • • •

*NOT WHAT EVERYONE ELSE
THINKS YOU SHOULD HAVE.*

• • • • • • • • • • • • • • • • • • • •

(Might be worth letting your partner
have an opinion, though …)

They dream in courtship,
but in wedlock wake.

Alexander Pope

GOOD MORNING!

To everyone except

those guests that

DON'T
RSVP

on time.

STAGES OF CHOOSING YOUR WEDDING VENUE

STAGE ONE

Manor House! With a garden!
And a lake!

STAGE TWO

That costs **HOW MUCH?!**

STAGE THREE

Okay, maybe a marquee on a lawn?

STAGE FOUR

Sorry, how much ...?

STAGE FIVE

Tent. We're gonna have to squeeze
100 guests into a pop-up tent.

We loved with a love
that was more than love.

Edgar Allan Poe
Annabel Lee

Turns out
we're planning
two weddings ...

the one inspired by

Pinterest and

the one we can

ACTUALLY AFFORD.

Oh s**t,
there's a wasp
in my bouquet!

No, I can't make my wedding cake gluten free for you.

#sorrynotsorry

**Life is the flower for
which love is the honey.**

Victor Hugo

It's possible I'll be the first one to leave our wedding reception.

I need to sleep for a year after all this planning ...

Two hearts in love
need no words.

Marceline Desbordes-Valmore

I'll climb every
mountain with you.

In the end,

it's not going to

matter how many

breaths you took,

but how many moments

took your breath away.

Shing Xiong

Two souls with but
a single thought,

Two hearts
that beat as one.

John Keats

If it isn't sunny on my wedding day I'm not turning up.

Marriage

is the highest state of

FRIENDSHIP.

Samuel Richardson

I can't wait
for my
hay fever to
really kick
in on my
wedding day ...

Relationships are like a walk in the park.

Jurassic Park.

HOW NOT TO WRITE YOUR WEDDING SPEECH

By giving it to someone else to write.

Stealing it from a website word-for-word. Not cool.

The night before your wedding. No one needs that kind of stress.

In the car on the way to the ceremony ... *SERIOUSLY?!*

While you're actually giving your speech. No. Just, **NO.**

You are my today
and all of my tomorrows.

You will forever
be my always.

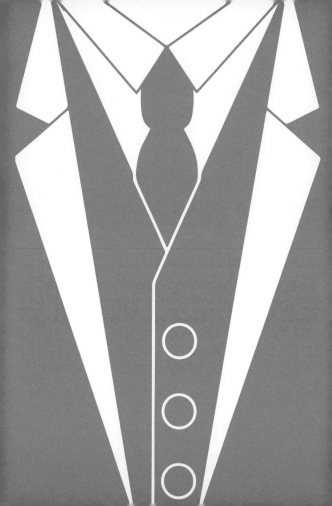

My most brilliant achievement
was my ability to be able to
persuade my wife to marry me.

Winston Churchill

Marriage is popular

because it combines

the maximum of

temptation

with the maximum of

opportunity.

George Bernard Shaw

Married Sexting:
Guess what ... I'm not wearing any underwear because you didn't put the f**king laundry in the dryer like I asked you to 100 times.
...

What counts in making
a happy marriage is not
so much how compatible
you are, but how you deal
with incompatibility.

Leo Tolstoy

I vow to always be the
mac to your cheese.